760
789
Ful
c. 1

Fuller, Catherine Leuthold
Beasts, an alphabet of
fine prints

Date Due

DORR H 1 02 2'79		
BIGS H 11 22 83		

Twenty-six prints of animals which each
represent a letter of the alphabet. Includes
a brief survey of the history of printmaking.

BEASTS

AN ALPHABET OF FINE PRINTS

BEASTS

AN ALPHABET OF FINE PRINTS

Selected by

CATHERINE LEUTHOLD FULLER

Boston   LITTLE, BROWN AND COMPANY   Toronto

Published simultaneously in Canada
by Little, Brown & Company (Canada) Limited

PRINTED IN THE UNITED STATES OF AMERICA

Introduction

BEASTS: *An Alphabet of Fine Prints* is intended to please young people, to develop keen observation, and to enable them to make friends with some fine examples of graphic art. On a visit to an art museum children may pass an equestrian statue or stroll through a garden court decorated with sculpture. In the galleries they may meet a charming little girl painted by Renoir, or be puzzled, yet enthralled, by an imposing religious scene by Zurbarán. But the small and often intricately designed Old Master prints on exhibition in a museum cannot be enjoyed by children as well as their parents because the prints must be hung at a height to accommodate adults. Thus Rodin's *Thinker* and portraits by Rembrandt may become familiar to young people, yet fine prints may still be unknown to them.

The reproductions of engravings, etchings, woodcuts, and lithographs in this book can be examined closely, just as the artists intended the originals to be scrutinized. When children grow older, and taller, they may study actual impressions in an exhibition gallery or in a print room, where the artists' mastery of technique, the craftsmanship of the printing, and the subtle texture of the paper can be appreciated as well as the beauty of the composition.

An alphabet illustrated with Old Master prints was first thought of in the Department of Prints and Drawings of the Cleveland Museum of Art many years ago while a study was being made of the engravings of Lucas van Leyden and his sixteenth-century contemporaries. Early engravings abound with captivating beasts, birds, and insects. To choose twenty-six from the enormous number of prints made by Europeans and Americans from the fifteenth century to the present day has been a lively challenge.

I restricted my selection to prints from the Cleveland Museum of Art and the Achenbach Foundation for Graphic Arts, San Francisco, because these collections were immediately available to me and offered an abundance of examples of superb quality. To have drawn on other sources would have only complicated the selection unduly. The very nature of the graphic arts, offering multiple originals, tremendous quantity and diversity, meant that standards and limitations had to be set.

Obviously, the letters of our alphabet establish the framework of the selection. But, for example, there are too many D's to choose from: dogs, deer, donkeys are overwhelmingly abundant. On the other hand, there is an embarrassing scarcity of N's: nightingales and newts did not inspire printmakers. And A, except for the humble and very familiar beast in the Flight into Egypt, offered surprisingly few candidates. Some splendid creatures were omitted because the main subject was a gruesome martyrdom, or the iconography was extremely difficult to understand. Certain prints left no other choice: the fifteenth-century Italian elephant; Lucas van Leyden's cow; Baldung's horse; Dürer's monkey. Quality was my criterion, defined in several ways. Each print was rated by these standards: its merit as a work of art; the technical excellence of the particular impression; the suitability of the subject matter; the clarity of the detail chosen for enlargement; the compatibility of the design with the others chosen for the book; its usefulness in meeting problems of vocabulary; its importance in the history of the graphic arts. Some meet every requirement; for example, the quartet of the Master E. S., Jean Duvet, Francisco Goya, and William Blake. In other instances, weights had to be awarded, for lesser artists adorned their periods as they do this alphabet.

To try to cover the entire history of printmaking in a book for children would seem to be folly. Books about the history of graphic art and techniques are listed in the bibliography which appears at the end of this book. The twenty-six prints chosen for this alphabet are worth knowing, and the wide gaps can be filled by further study. There is no text other than the formal cataloguing because each print will, it is hoped, suggest a story to an imaginative young person. Our intention is not to burden him with complicated iconography, but rather to let him see and enjoy pictures which are part of the artistic heritage of Western civilization.

Three masterpieces of engraving represent the fifteenth century. In the north of Europe the Gothic style prevailed, and engraving was closely allied with the art of the goldsmiths, as illustrated by the *St. John the Baptist in the Desert* (I) of 1466, by a goldsmith-engraver known only as the Master E. S., who worked in southern Germany and Switzerland. The fifteenth-century Italian Renaissance also produced engravings that are great works of art, such as *The Triumph of Caesar: The Elephants* (E) by an unknown artist of the School of Andrea Mantegna. Scholars are uncertain of the purpose for which the famous so-called *Tarocchi* (playing cards) were engraved, but *The Gentleman, Ranks and Conditions of Men* (F) typifies their charm.

The sixteenth-century Renaissance in northern Europe was dominated by Albrecht Dürer, whose woodcuts and engravings exerted an enormous influence throughout Europe. His *Virgin and Child with a Monkey* (M) of about 1498 is magnificent in every way, and the monkey is without equal. It was difficult to decide on the one best lion, but the handsome sixteenth-century specimen in Dürer's *St. Jerome in His Study* (L) of 1514 won over a large field of contenders. *The Milkmaid* (C) of 1510 is a masterly study of peasant life by Lucas van Leyden of the Netherlands. His genius was entirely different from Dürer's, and only in the rare, early impressions can his subtle, delicate rendering of atmosphere and the effect of distance be appreciated. A number of German artists, strongly influenced by Dürer, are called the Little Masters because their prints are small. *Rabbits Roasting a Hunter and His Dog* (R) is a fantasy by Virgil Solis of Nuremberg, who began in the style of the Little Masters, although he is not considered one of them. The designs of ornament, intended to be used by goldsmiths and armorers, are fascinating. Our example (O), elegantly combining snails, butterflies, caterpillars, owls, foliage, and other forms, is by Theodor de Bry, a Fleming who migrated to Frankfurt and who also worked in London.

A very great treasure of Cleveland's Print Room is the set of illustrations engraved by the French mystic Jean Duvet for *The Apocalypse.* His seven-headed beast (N) very clearly is based on Dürer's, from his woodcut *Apocalypse* of 1498, but Duvet has endowed his beast with a much more intense personality.

Although single woodcuts from the fifteenth century have survived, they are often in poor condition and frequently their iconography is of a strongly religious nature that is not suitable for this alphabet. Indeed, fifteenth-century woodcuts are so directly concerned with the complexities of early book illustration that none appears here. Our earliest is an exceptionally fine impression of a German woodcut from the second quarter of the sixteenth century, *The Bewitched Groom* (H), by Hans Baldung (called Grien). The theme of magic and witchcraft is combined with a Renaissance interest in representation according to the rules of perspective. The page from the rare book of 1592 (V), engraved by Jacob Hoefnagel when he was seventeen after drawings by his father, serves as a signpost to mark the decline of the woodcut for book illustration: the demand for finer detail in the cutting of the block had created difficulties in printing that could not then be solved.

The engraver in the seventeenth century very often ceased to be a creative artist and became a technically skilled craftsman who reproduced the work of painters and other artists. Rubens, a good businessman, even employed his own engravers to reproduce his paintings and spread his fame. Printsellers commissioned and published large editions of prints to satisfy the popular demand for pictures, and huge collections were assembled. In the eighteenth century Hogarth made engravings after his own paintings, and he received more income from the sale of the prints than from the sale of a single painting. Investing in prints by the public became highly fashionable.

The creation of the animals, Noah's ark, and the legend of Orpheus are subjects favored by artists who wish to depict the world of nature. *Orpheus Enchanting the Birds and Animals* (P), by Antonio Tempesta, is a beguiling hodge-podge of real and imaginary animals. Sleeker parrots exist in designs by other artists, but this bird probably was of the loquacious variety. Tempesta, an Italian of slight talent, produced a tremendous number of prints which were widely distributed in the late sixteenth and early seventeenth centuries. Instead of the slow, precise method of engraving, he preferred the quicker technique of etching.

No master of the seventeenth or eighteenth century is represented in this alphabet. Rembrandt in the seventeenth century brought etching to its highest point. Occasionally he drew raffish dogs, but for our present purpose at least, even his lovely lion in *St. Jerome Reading in an Italian Landscape* does not match Dürer's sixteenth-century beauty. The grandeur of the Baroque and the sophisticated elegancies and allegories of the eighteenth century are out of place in this book, intended to provide young people with a small circle of friends in the graphic arts. Rembrandt, Callot, and their contemporaries, the whole area of portraiture, the eighteenth century of Tiepolo, Canaletto, Piranesi, the French line engravers, and the English mezzotinters may be studied later. The joy of making new discoveries will always reward the inquisitive mind.

In England at the end of the eighteenth century lived William Blake, a mystic of independent spirit, a poet, an artist, and the inventor of the technique of relief etching. Blake engraved his masterpiece, the *Illustrations of the Book of Job*, in his last years. The page (X) reproduced here shows the power and originality of Blake's imagination. The graphic work of the Spanish genius, Francisco Goya, also belongs to the end of the eighteenth century and the early nineteenth. Goya used etching and the new technique of aquatint with marvelous effect, as shown by *A Way of Flying* (Q), and late in his life he produced masterpieces of lithography.

The nineteenth century was a time of tremendous social upheaval. With the end of the old aristocracy in France a different class appeared as patrons of art. There was a demand for more pictures and less expensive ones; the new medium of lithography, invented in Bavaria by Aloys Senefelder, began to attract artists who experimented with its possibilities. Among the incunabula of lithography is *Mountain Landscape with Bear* (U) by Maximilian Josef Wagenbauer. The French Romanticists often portrayed wild animals fighting viciously or attacking their prey. In a more lighthearted mood, *Young Tiger Playing with Its Mother* (T) of 1831 indicates that Eugène Delacroix was a master of lithography. In Germany, Adolph Menzel also brought lithography to a high degree of excellence. *The Bear Pit* (B) of 1851 is from his well-known series *Experiments on Stone with Brush and Scraper (Versuche auf Stein mit Pinsel und Schabeisen)*.

In the middle of the nineteenth century Charles Meryon, one of the greatest masters of etching, produced his magnificent studies of the architectural beauties of Paris. *The Gallery of Notre Dame, Paris* (J) of 1853 is from this famous series, *Etchings of Paris (Eaux-fortes sur Paris)*. Meryon was among the artists and writers who, together with a publisher and a printer, formed the Society of Etchers (*Société des Aquafortistes*) in 1862 in France. The concern of this group was to free printmaking from the bondage of commercial reproductive work. A leader in this movement was Félix Bracquemond, who is remembered especially for his encouragement of younger artists. *The Unknown* (D) is from the first publication by the Society of Etchers and shows that Bracquemond observed nature closely and could etch with skill.

Consider now what happened to woodcut. In the seventeenth and eighteenth centuries this medium was still used to illustrate exciting events, but these pictures were crudely executed and had little artistic merit. At the end of the eighteenth century Thomas Bewick exploited wood engraving, and his tiny scenes of English country life are technically excellent. By the middle of the nineteenth century wood engraving reached its lowest point as a medium for original work, although craftsmen of remarkable skill reproduced paintings and drawings for publications. *The Cuvier-Chatillon Rock* (W) of 1887, drawn and engraved by Auguste Lepère, indicates a turning point in the history of woodcut in France. Lepère, who was a commercial wood engraver, recognized that the new photomechanical processes would supplant reproductive wood engraving. He joined in the effort to emphasize line again in wood engraving rather than tone. In the early twentieth century the German Expressionists made dramatic woodcuts.

Much important graphic work by the French Impressionists and Post-impressionists is in color and outside the scope of this alphabet, but Paul Gauguin's *Pastoral Scene, Martinique* (G) of about 1889 is a splendid lithograph on zinc to represent the achievement of these artists. Their work was not widely accepted when it appeared and was appreciated only by the discriminating eye.

The British etchers of the nineteenth and early twentieth centuries followed the lead of Sir Francis Seymour Haden, who based his style on the landscape etchings of Rembrandt. Although now somewhat out of fashion, the work of these men, among them Sir Muirhead Bone, Edmund

Blampied, and David Young Cameron, has been popular and widely collected. The American Frank W. Benson came under this influence, and *Yellowlegs No. 2* (Y) of 1919 is typical of his manner. In the 1930's, many American artists depicted life in their own regions. *The Circus* (Z) of 1932, by Henry G. Keller, whose studies of birds and animals form a handsome group of prints, catches the atmosphere of the days of the Big Top.

The twentieth-century movements in art, such as Cubism and Surrealism, and the activities of groups such as The Bridge (*Die Brücke*) and The Blue Rider (*Der blaue Reiter*) are vigorously expressed in printmaking by innovations in subject matter and a continuing technical experimentation. Joseph Hecht, who worked in Paris, concerned himself particularly with engraving. Although the antelope of India is spotted only in Hecht's imagination, *Asia* (A) is a lively example of his style. His *Australia* (K) of about 1925 gives a fanciful idea of the interior of this continent. *Les livres de peintres* is a phrase often used to describe handsomely designed and printed books containing original works of graphic art by great masters. Ambroise Vollard, who is credited with starting this important phase of book publishing and printmaking in the late nineteenth century, commissioned André Dunoyer de Segonzac to illustrate Virgil's *Georgics*. These lyrical scenes of the French countryside (S) were etched directly from nature with an astonishing sureness. Because of the death of Vollard, the book was published later by the artist.

Our circle of friends is now complete but not closed; it will become ever wider as new discoveries are made in the fascinating world of the graphic arts.

BEASTS

AN ALPHABET OF FINE PRINTS

Antelope

ASIA
from the set "Five Continents" in the *Atlas*

Engraving by Joseph Hecht
Polish-French, 1891–1951
Achenbach Foundation for Graphic Arts, San Francisco

3

B

Bear

THE BEAR PIT

Lithograph
by Adolph Friedrich Erdmann von Menzel
German, 1815–1905
The Cleveland Museum of Art
Mr. and Mrs. Lewis B. Williams Collection

C

Cow

THE MILKMAID

Engraving by Lucas van Leyden
Dutch, 1494(?)–1533
The Cleveland Museum of Art
Leonard C. Hanna Jr. Collection

7

D

Duck

THE UNKNOWN

Etching and drypoint by Félix Bracquemond
French, 1833–1914
The Cleveland Museum of Art
Mr. and Mrs. Charles G. Prasse Collection
Gift of Leona E. Prasse

E

Elephant

THE TRIUMPH OF CAESAR: THE ELEPHANTS

Engraving by an artist of the School of Andrea Mantegna
Italian, late fifteenth century
Private collection, San Francisco

F

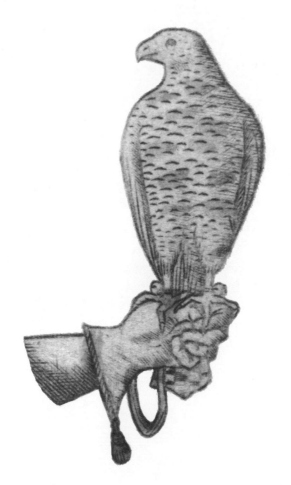

Falcon

THE GENTLEMAN, RANKS AND CONDITIONS OF MEN
from the so-called *Tarocchi* (playing cards)

Engraving by an unknown artist
North Italian, about 1460–1467
The Cleveland Museum of Art
Dudley P. Allen Fund

13

G

Goat

PASTORAL SCENE, MARTINIQUE

Lithograph on zinc by Paul Gauguin
French, 1848–1903
The Cleveland Museum of Art
Dudley P. Allen Fund

15

H

Horse

17

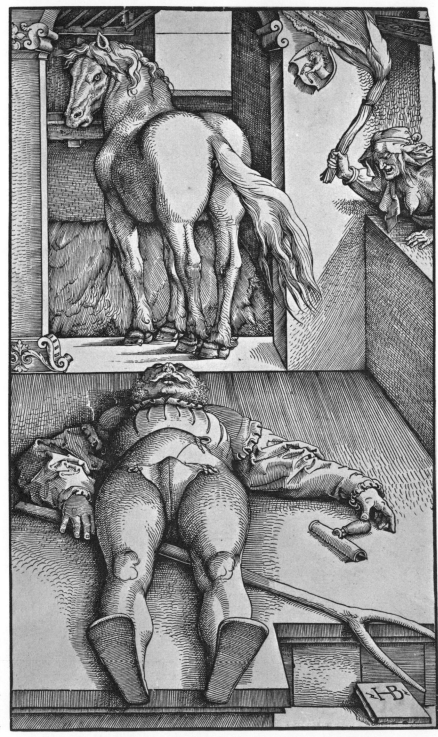

THE BEWITCHED GROOM

Woodcut by Hans Baldung (called Grien)
German, 1484/5–1545
The Cleveland Museum of Art
Mr. and Mrs. Charles G. Prasse Collection
Fiftieth Anniversary Gift

I

Imaginary Ox

19

ST. JOHN THE BAPTIST IN THE DESERT
Surrounded by the Symbols of the Evangelists
and the Four Fathers of the Latin Church

Engraving by the Master E. S.
German, active about 1450 to 1470
The Cleveland Museum of Art
John L. Severance Fund

J

Jackdaw

THE GALLERY OF NOTRE DAME, PARIS

Etching by Charles Meryon
French, 1821–1868
The Cleveland Museum of Art
The Milton Curtiss Rose Collection

K

Kangaroo

AUSTRALIA
from the set "Five Continents" in the *Atlas*

Engraving by Joseph Hecht
Polish-French, 1891–1951
Achenbach Foundation for Graphic Arts, San Francisco

L

Lion

ST. JEROME IN HIS STUDY

Engraving by Albrecht Dürer
German, 1471–1528
The Cleveland Museum of Art
Leonard C. Hanna Jr. Collection

M

Monkey

VIRGIN AND CHILD WITH A MONKEY

Engraving by Albrecht Dürer
German, 1471–1528
The Cleveland Museum of Art
Dudley P. Allen Fund

N

Nonesuch Beast

HEC HISTORIA·
APOCALIPSIS·
CAP · I Ƨ·

THE WOMAN CLOTHED WITH THE SUN
from *The Apocalypse*

Engraving by Jean Duvet
French, about 1485–after 1556
The Cleveland Museum of Art
Gift of Hanna Fund

Owl

ORNAMENT

Engraving by Theodor de Bry
Flemish-German, 1528–1598
The Cleveland Museum of Art
Gift of The Print Club of Cleveland

31

P

Parrot

Vt uolucres cantuq feras Rodopeius Orpheus
Dicitur et dulci detinuisse lyra

Sic animos tu Sannesi dulcedine morum
Allicis, obstrictos et facis esse tibi

ILL.ᵈᵈ IACOBO SANNESIO SACRÆ
CONSVLTÆ AVD ET SECR DIGN.
Antonius Tempesta D.D.

Quis neget en ipsa trahis Orphea cuncta trahentē
Aspice, stas mutus nec sonat ipsa chelis
Dominicus de Rubeis formis Romæ ad Templum Pacis

Obstupuit laudum perculsus amore tuarum
Sic tamen et laudes spirat imago tuas.

ORPHEUS ENCHANTING THE BIRDS AND ANIMALS

Etching by Antonio Tempesta
Italian, 1555–1630
Achenbach Foundation for Graphic Arts, San Francisco

33

Queer Bird

A WAY OF FLYING
from *The Proverbs*

Etching, aquatint, and drypoint (?)
by Francisco José de Goya y Lucientes
Spanish, 1746–1828
Achenbach Foundation for Graphic Arts, San Francisco

35

R

Rabbit

RABBITS ROASTING A HUNTER AND HIS DOG

Engraving by Virgil Solis
German, 1514–1562
The Cleveland Museum of Art
Gift of The Print Club of Cleveland

S

Sheep

Illustration for Virgil's *Georgics*

Etching by
André Dunoyer de Segonzac
French, 1884—
The Cleveland Museum of Art
Gift of Hanna Fund

T

Tiger

Etig. Delacroix.   Lith. de Delaunois.

Jeune Tigre jouant avec sa mère

YOUNG TIGER PLAYING WITH ITS MOTHER

Lithograph by Ferdinand Victor Eugène Delacroix
French, 1798–1863
Achenbach Foundation for Graphic Arts, San Francisco

41

U

Urchin
or Hedgehog

MOUNTAIN LANDSCAPE WITH BEAR

Lithograph by Maximilian Josef Wagenbauer
German, 1774–1829
The Cleveland Museum of Art
Mr. and Mrs. Lewis B. Williams Collection

V

Viper

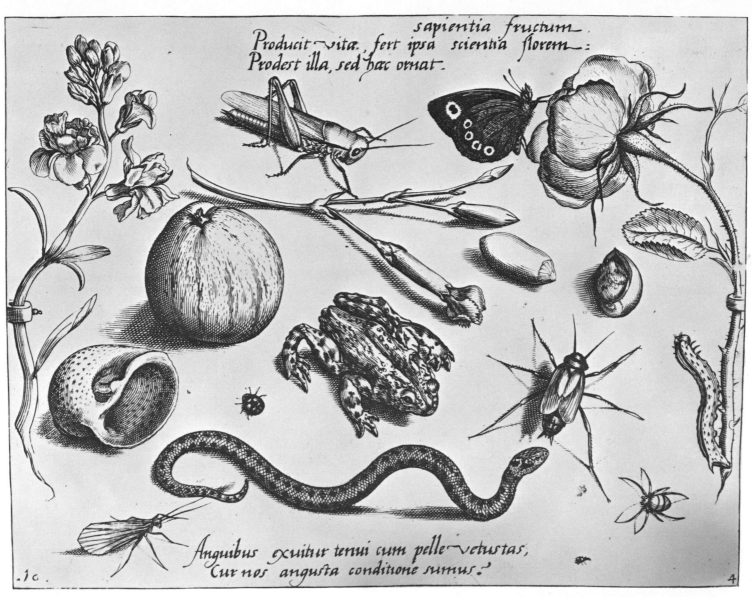

sapientia fructum
Producit vita, fert ipsa scientia florem:
Prodest illa, sed hæc ornat.

Anguibus exuitur tenui cum pelle vetustas,
Cur nos angusta conditione sumus?

.10.

4

Page from *Archetypa Studiaque Patris Georgii Hoefnagelii* . . .

Engraving by Jacob Hoefnagel
Flemish, 1575–1630
Achenbach Foundation for Graphic Arts, San Francisco

W

Wild Boar

47

THE CUVIER-CHATILLON ROCK
from the series, *The Forest of Fontainebleau*

Wood engraving by
Louis Auguste Lepère
French, 1849–1918
Achenbach Foundation for Graphic Arts, San Francisco

eXtraordinary Animal

49

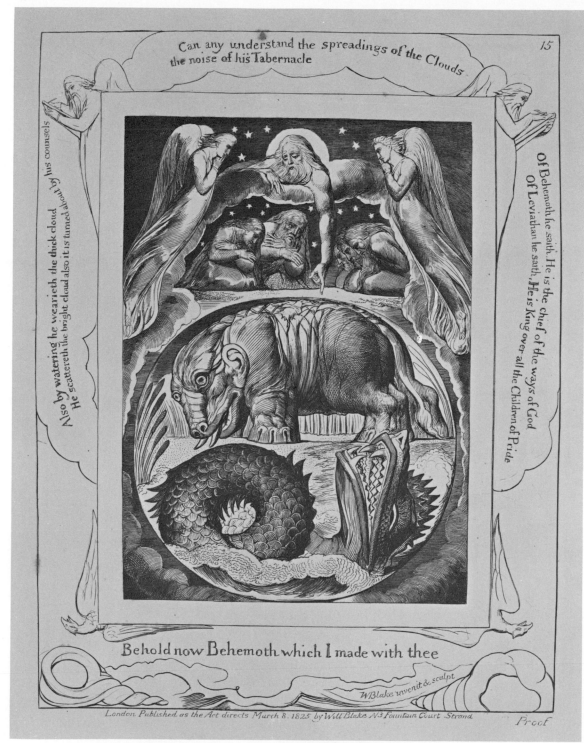

Engraving from
Illustrations of the Book of Job
by William Blake
English, 1757–1827
The Cleveland Museum of Art
Mr. and Mrs. Charles G. Prasse Collection
Gift of Leona E. Prasse

Y

Yellowlegs

YELLOWLEGS No. 2

Drypoint by Frank Weston Benson
American, 1862–1951
The Cleveland Museum of Art
Leonard C. Hanna Jr. Collection

Z

Zebra

CIRCUS

Lithograph by Henry G. Keller
American, 1869–1949
The Cleveland Museum of Art
Gift of The Cleveland Print Makers

Acknowledgments

This book evolved from discussions with many people. My debt to all who looked, considered, and offered opinions is immense.

Without the generous assistance and encouragement of the staff of the Department of Prints and Drawings, The Cleveland Museum of Art, this book would not have come into being. In particular, Miss Leona E. Prasse and Miss Louise S. Richards gave much needed counsel. I am also grateful for the guidance of Dr. Merald E. Wrolstad, editor of museum publications.

At the Achenbach Foundation for Graphic Arts, California Palace of the Legion of Honor, San Francisco, I wish to thank the director, Dr. E. Gunter Troche, Mr. Fenton Kastner, Mr. Dennis Beall, and Mrs. David Jamison McDaniel for many valuable contributions and for thoughtful criticisms.

At the California Academy of Sciences, San Francisco, Dr. Robert T. Orr, associate director, and Dr. Edward S. Ross, chairman of the Department of Entomology, gave me much helpful advice and suggestions for proper terminology.

The final revisions were made in Melbourne, Australia. I am grateful to the staff of both the Art Library, State Library of Victoria, and the Department of Prints and Drawings, National Gallery of Victoria, and in particular, Mr. Harley Preston, for friendly cooperation and assistance.

Above all, to my husband, who is patient, I owe my deepest gratitude.

C. L. F.

A Brief Bibliography

Several books on the history of graphic art are listed here. *The Book of Fine Prints* by Carl Zigrosser is the most comprehensive, and all periods and techniques are discussed. It also contains an annotated bibliography. As its title suggests, the book by David Bland covers the history of a field in which the graphic arts play an important part. In the Index under the name of each artist, a more detailed, scholarly reference has been given whenever one was available.

The actual process of creating an original print may be as simple as making a linoleum block, or much technical knowledge and exacting craftsmanship in the execution of the plate and in its actual printing may be involved. The second section of the bibliography lists books which describe the relief, intaglio, and planographic processes and the so-called mixed media, and which also provide glossaries of terms used in printmaking. The book by Felix Brunner shows how complicated modern industrial technology has made the field of graphic art. A comparison of the enlargements in William M. Ivins's *How Prints Look* with the reproductions in this alphabet would be an excellent preparation for examining original prints in a print room to make clear the difference between an engraving, etching, woodcut, or lithograph and a reproduction. Because the history of paper-making is closely related to the history of printmaking, the book by Dard Hunter *Papermaking* is included.

HISTORY OF PRINTS

Bland, David. *A History of Book Illustration: The Illuminated Manuscript and the Printed Book.* Cleveland and New York, 1958.

Hind, Arthur M. *A History of Engraving and Etching.* London, 1923. Paperback edition: New York, 1963.

Weber, Wilhelm. *A History of Lithography.* London, 1966.

Zigrosser, Carl. *The Book of Fine Prints.* New York, 1948.

HISTORY OF PRINTS (*Continued*)

The catalogues of three important exhibitions provide a survey of the history of printmaking:

The First Century of Printmaking, 1400–1500. A Catalogue Compiled by Elizabeth Mongan and Carl O. Schniewind. An Exhibition at The Art Institute of Chicago . . . 1941.

Prints 1400–1800. A Loan Exhibition from Museums and Private Collections . . . The Minneapolis Institute of Arts, 1956.

Prints 1800–1945. A Loan Exhibition from Museums and Private Collections . . . The Minneapolis Institute of Arts, 1966.

PRINTMAKING TECHNIQUES AND PAPERMAKING

Brunner, Felix. *A Handbook of Graphic Reproduction Processes.* Teufen (Switzerland), 1962.

Hayter, Stanley W. *About Prints.* London, 1962.

Hunter, Dard. *Papermaking: The History and Technique of an Ancient Craft.* New York, 1947.

Ivins, William M., Jr. *How Prints Look.* New York, 1943. Paperback edition: Boston, 1960.

Lumsden, Ernest S. *The Art of Etching.* London, 1925. Paperback edition: New York, 1962.

Peterdi, Gabor. *Printmaking.* New York, 1959.

Zigrosser, Carl, and Christa M. Gaehde. *A Guide to the Collecting and Care of Original Prints.* New York, 1965.

Index of Sources

To complete the information about each print reproduced in the alphabet, a reference to a *catalogue raisonné* or other definitive scholarly work, if available, is given under the name of the artist. The dimensions give height before width.

Page Number

Baldung, Hans (called Grien).
    The Bewitched Groom. 342 x 200 mm. No. 77, page 279 *in* (exhibition catalogue) *Hans Baldung Grien* (Karlsruhe: Staatliche Kunsthalle, 1959)   17

Benson, Frank Weston
    Yellowlegs No. 2. 200 x 250 mm. No. 162 *in* Adam Edwin Merriman Paff, *Etchings and Drypoints by Frank W. Benson,* Vol. III (Boston and New York, 1923)   51

Blake, William
    Plate 15 from *Illustrations of the Book of Job.* 197 x 149 mm. No. 120, II/II, *in* Laurence Binyon, *The Engraved Designs of William Blake* (London and New York, 1926)   49

Bracquemond, Félix
    The Unknown. 137 x 282 mm. No. 174, III/III, *in* Henri Beraldi, *Les graveurs du XIXe siècle,* Vol. III (Paris, 1885)   9

Bry, Theodor de
    Ornament. 97 x 75 mm. No. 195 *in* F. W. H. Hollstein, *Dutch and Flemish Etchings, Engravings and Woodcuts,* Vol. IV (Amsterdam, n.d.)   31

Delacroix, Ferdinand Victor Eugène
    Young Tiger Playing with Its Mother. 112 x 187 mm. No. 91, I/VI, *in* Loys Delteil, *Le peintre-graveur illustré,* Vol. III (Paris, 1908)   41

Dunoyer de Segonzac, André
    The Sheep, Plain of Cogolin, illustration for *Virgile: Les Géorgiques* . . .
    illustrées d'eaux-fortes par Dunoyer de Segonzac (Paris, 1947). 292 x 244
    mm. No. 938 *in* Aimée Lioré and Pierre Cailler, *Catalogue de l'oeuvre*
    gravé de Dunoyer de Segonzac, Vol. V (Geneva, 1965)   39

Dürer, Albrecht
    St. Jerome in His Study. 248 x 190 mm. No. 59 *in* Joseph Meder,
    Dürer-Katalog (Vienna, 1932)   25

Dürer, Albrecht
    Virgin and Child with a Monkey. 191 x 122 mm. No. 30, proof a, *in*
    Meder, *ibid.*   27

Duvet, Jean
    The Woman Clothed with the Sun, illustration for *L'Apocalypse figurée* . . .
    (Lyons, 1561). 298 x 211 mm. No. 38 *in* A. P. F. Robert-Dumesnil,
    Le peintre-graveur français, Vol. V (Paris, 1841)   29

Gauguin, Paul
    Pastoral Scene, Martinique. 213 x 263 mm. No. 9 *in* Marcel Guérin,
    L'oeuvre gravé de Gauguin (Paris, 1927)   15

Goya y Lucientes, Francisco José de
    A Way of Flying, Plate 13 from the series, *The Proverbs.* 245 x 350 mm.
    No. 260, III, first edition, 1864 *in* Tomás Harris, *Goya: Engravings*
    and Lithographs, Vol. II (Oxford, 1964)   35

Hecht, Joseph
    Asia, from the set "Five Continents" in the *Atlas.* 199 x 295 mm.   3

Hecht, Joseph
    Australia, from the set "Five Continents" in the *Atlas.* 238 x 339 mm.   23

Hoefnagel, Jacob
    Plate 10, Volume IV of *Archetypa Studiaque Patris Georgii Hoefnagelii* . . .
    (Frankfurt-on-Main, 1592). About 159 x 208 mm. No. 62 *in* F. W.
    H. Hollstein, *Dutch and Flemish Etchings Engravings and Woodcuts,* Vol.
    IX (Amsterdam, n.d.)   45

Keller, Henry G.
    Circus. 294 x 444 mm.   53

Lepère, Louis Auguste
    The Cuvier-Chatillon Rock from the series, *The Forest of Fontainebleau.*

216 x 163 mm. No. 158 *in* A. Lotz-Brissonneau, *Catalogue de l'oeuvre gravé de Auguste Lepère* (Paris, 1905)   47

Leyden, Lucas van
   The Milkmaid. 115 x 156 mm. No. 158 *in* Eugène Dutuit, *Manuel de l'amateur d'estampes: Ecoles flamande et hollandaise,* Vol. V (Paris and London, 1882)   7

Master E. S.
   St. John the Baptist in the Desert . . . 182 mm. to border. No. 149, I/II *in* Max Lehrs, *Geschichte und kritischer Katalog des deutschen, niederländischen und französischen Kupferstichs im XV. Jahrhundert,* Vol. II (Vienna, 1910)   19

Menzel, Adolph Friedrich Erdmann von
   The Bear Pit. 248 x 197 mm. No. 404, III/III, *in* Elfried Bock, *Adolph Menzel: Verzeichnis seines graphischen Werkes* (Berlin, 1923)   5

Meryon, Charles
   The Gallery of Notre Dame, Paris. 283 x 175 mm. No. 26, III/V, *in* Loys Delteil, edited by Harold J. L. Wright, *Catalogue Raisonné of the Etchings of Charles Meryon* (New York, 1924)   21

North Italian, about 1460–1467
   The Gentleman, Ranks and Conditions of Men from the so-called *Tarocchi* (playing cards). About 180 x 102 mm. No. E.I.5,a, page 234, *in* Arthur M. Hind, *Early Italian Engraving,* Pt. I, Vol. I (London, 1938)   13

School of Andrea Mantegna
   The Triumph of Caesar: The Elephants. About 290 x 263 mm. No. 14, page 22, *in* Arthur M. Hind, *Early Italian Engraving,* Pt. II, Vol. V (London, 1948)   11

Solis, Virgil
   Rabbits Roasting a Hunter and His Dog. 25 x 202 mm. No. 271 *in* Adam Bartsch, *Le peintre graveur,* Vol. IX (Vienna, 1808)   37

Tempesta, Antonio
   Orpheus Enchanting the Birds and Animals. 338 x 448 mm. No. 826 *in* Adam Bartsch, *Le peintre graveur,* Vol. XVII (Vienna, 1818)   33

Wagenbauer, Maximilian Josef
   Mountain Landscape with Bear. 227 x 356 mm. No. 43, page 282, *in* Luitpold Dussler, *Die Incunabeln der deutschen Lithographie* (Berlin, 1925)   43